# When My Sister Got Sick

# KIDS HAVE *TROUBLES* TOO

# When My Sister
# Got Sick

by Sheila Stewart and Rae Simons

Mason Crest Publishers

MASON CREST PUBLISHERS INC.
370 Reed Road
Broomall, Pennsylvania 19008
(866)MCP-BOOK (toll free)
www.masoncrest.com

First Printing
9 8 7 6 5 4 3 2 1

    CIP data on file with the Library of Congress

 ISBN (set) 978-1-4222-1691-0    ISBN 978-1-4222-1702-3
 ISBN (ppbk set) 978-1-4222-1904-1    ISBN 978-1-4222-1915-7    (pbk.)


Design by MK Bassett-Harvey.
Produced by Harding House Publishing Service, Inc.
www.hardinghousepages.com
Cover design by Torque Advertising + Design.
Printed in USA by Bang Printing.

The creators of this book have made every effort to provide accurate information, but it should not be used as a substitute for the help and services of trained professionals.

# Introduction

Each child is unique—and each child encounters a unique set of circumstances in life. Some of these circumstances are more challenging than others, and how a child copes with those challenges will depend in large part on the other resources in her life.

The issues children encounter cover a wide range. Some of these are common to almost all children, including threats to self-esteem, anger management, and learning to identify emotions. Others are more unique to individual families, but problems such as parental unemployment, a death in the family, or divorce and remarriage are common but traumatic events in many children's lives. Still others—like domestic abuse, alcoholism, and the incarceration of a family member—are unfortunately not uncommon in today's world.

Whatever problems a child encounters in life, understanding that he is not alone is a key component to helping him cope. These books, both their fiction and nonfiction elements, allow children to see that other children are in the same situations. The books make excellent tools for triggering conversation in a nonthreatening way. They will also promote understanding and compassion in children who may not be experiencing these issues themselves.

These books offer children important factual information—but perhaps more important, they offer hope.

*—Cindy Croft, M.A., Ed., Director of the Center for Inclusive Child Care*

"What are we going to do for my birthday this year?" Keiko asked her mother when she got in the car after school. "Jodie wants to know if I'm having a party."

Keiko waited for her mother to say something. Her mom just drove, though, her eyes on the street in front of her.

"So am I?" Keiko asked. "I was thinking maybe I could have a tea party, the way Aimi did last year. We could all wear dress-up clothes and fancy hats and lots of jewelry."

She waited again for her mother to say something, but her mom was still quiet. Mom had a little frown between her eyebrows, though. Maybe she had a headache, Keiko thought. Maybe she was sad and worried about Keiko's big sister Aimi, the way Mom always was these days.

Maybe Keiko should just be quiet and not bother her mother.

But Keiko really needed to know about her birthday. After all, it was only two weeks away now. "Mom? Can I have a tea party for my birthday?"

Her mom shook her head, not so much like she was saying no, though. More like she was trying to wake herself up, or trying to shake the cobwebs out of her head. But then she shook her head again, and this time it looked like "no."

"I don't think so, Keiko. Not this year. Your birthday is only a couple of weeks away, and we don't know how Aimi will be doing. Even if she can be home by then, she'll still be having treatments. You know how sick those make her feel. I won't have time to plan a party—and we might end up just having to cancel it anyway, even if I did, if Aimi had another crisis." Her mother glanced sideways at Keiko and gave her a tiny smile, the kind of smile that meant "I'm sorry."

"Maybe next year, Keiko."

Keiko stared straight ahead through the windshield. They passed Jodie riding home from school on her bike, and Jodie waved, but Keiko couldn't bring herself to wave back. She felt as though something big and dark was piling up inside her, growing thicker and thicker, like a black cloud of ugly feelings that suddenly grew so big it burst out her mouth. "I'm tired of Aimi being sick!" she shouted.

Keiko expected her mom to yell at her, but she only sighed and kept driving. Her mother's face didn't even change. Maybe she hadn't even really heard Keiko at all.

Her mom's hair needed washing, Keiko noticed. In the old days, before Aimi got sick, Mom would have never looked all pale with stringy hair the way she did now. When Mom used to pick Keiko and Aimi up from school, she would be dressed in her work clothes, and she would look pretty. Now, she always wore jeans with one of Dad's baggy flannel shirts, as though she didn't really care what she looked like. Sometimes, she even forgot and wore her slippers when she went with Aimi to the hospital.

"Did you hear me, Mom?" Keiko said more loudly. "I'm tired of Aimi being sick all the time. It's not fair."

"No," Mom said in a tired voice. "It's not."

Keiko stared at her mother. That wasn't what she had expected her mother to say. She had thought her mother would be shocked. She'd thought her mom would yell at her. In a funny, angry sort of way, Keiko had even HOPED her mother would yell at her—and then Keiko would have yelled back, at the top of her lungs, and told her mother how awful it was to have parents who never noticed her anymore, who only thought about her sick big sister.

But now that her mother had agreed with her, Keiko didn't know what else to say. So she turned her head and watched the houses and trees as they went past the car window.

When they pulled into their driveway, her dad's truck wasn't parked by the garage the way it should have been. Keiko had known it wouldn't be there, but it still made her sad to see the empty place where it was usually parked after school. Today was Dad's turn to be at the hospital with Aimi, and he wouldn't come home until tomorrow.

Even the outside of the house looked different, Keiko thought as she got out of the car. The grass was longer, because Dad was too busy to mow it, and Mom hadn't bothered to plant the orange and yellow flowers along the sidewalk she usually did in the fall. The clubhouse where Keiko and Aimi had played all last summer looked sad and lonely.

Keiko followed Mom inside the house. The air smelled sad, she thought, like stale food and dirty laundry. The shadowy empty feeling made her shiver. Tears pricked the backs of her eyes, and then ran down her cheeks, but she turned her head away and hurried to her room before Mom could see. Mom looked too tired and sad herself to have to deal with Keiko's tears.

Life had started falling apart right after they went back to school after summer vacation. Aimi kept getting sick and having to miss school. At first it was just ordinary stuff, colds and an upset tummy, and Mom and Dad hadn't seemed very worried. And then one night, Keiko woke up in the night and heard Aimi crying in her room across the hall.

Aimi was two years older than Keiko, and she hardly ever cried anymore. Keiko thought maybe she was having a bad dream, but the crying didn't stop. It sounded funny too, like Aimi was wheezing and coughing at the same time that she was crying. Keiko got out of bed and went to the door of Aimi's room. "Aimi?" she whispered. "Are you okay?"

"Get Mom!" Aimi gasped. "I can't breathe."

Keiko ran down the hall and woke up her parents.

An hour later, they had all piled in the car and driven to the emergency room. By then, Aimi was starting to turn blue because she couldn't breathe.

Aimi and Keiko still had their pajamas on, Dad was wearing sweats, and Mom had on jeans with her nightgown tucked into the waistband. Keiko didn't like it that they weren't dressed right. It made everything seem more scary and wrong.

Mom rode in the back seat with Aimi, and Keiko was in the front seat with Dad. Her parents never let her ride in the front seat usually, so that wasn't right either. The night air still felt warm like summer, but Keiko couldn't stop shaking.

Her father kept glancing sideways and saying, "It's going to be all right, Keiko. Don't be scared." But Keiko thought he looked just as scared as she felt.

At the hospital, everything was very bright, as though inside the hospital it wasn't nighttime anymore. The doctors and nurses hooked up tubes and wires to Aimi's nose and chest and arm.

After a while, Aimi started being able to breathe normally again. Keiko heard both her parents sigh. Her mom put her arm around Keiko's shoulder, and then she gave a little laugh. "Whew! Let's not do that again, okay?"

Aimi had to stay overnight at the hospital, and Mom stayed with her, while Dad took Keiko home and put her back to bed just as the sky was starting to get light. The next day, Dad said Keiko didn't have to go school. They went out for breakfast instead, and then they went back to the hospital.

Keiko had thought that everything was going to go back to normal. Aimi had been sick again, worse this time, but now the doctors had given her medicine, and she was better. She would come home from the hospital and be fine.

But that's not what had happened. When they got to the hospital, Mom met them in the waiting room. "Aimi's sleeping," she said, but Keiko could tell just by looking at her that Mom was scared again, as scared as she'd been the night before

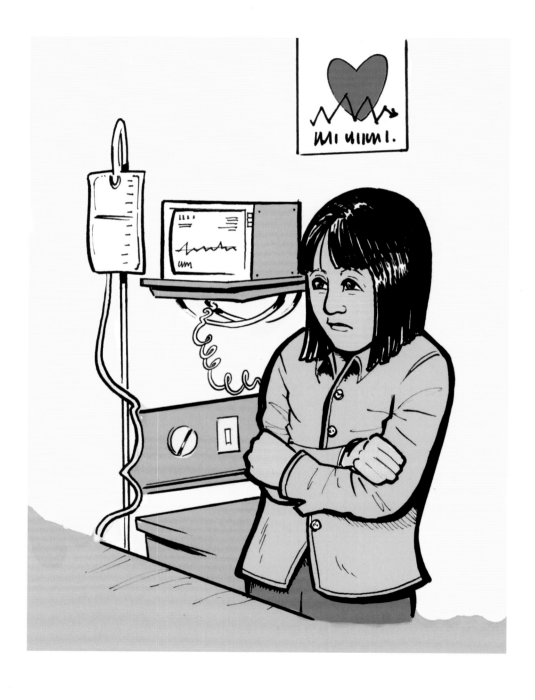

when Aimi couldn't breathe. "The doctor wants to talk to us," Mom said.

When they were all sitting down in the doctor's office, the doctor looked at them and said, "We think Aimi may have leukemia."

Keiko hadn't understood most of what the doctor had said that day. Later, her father had explained it to her. She understood now that leukemia was a kind of disease that meant the cells in Aimi's blood weren't normal and couldn't do their jobs. It was a bad disease, not like a cold or a tummy upset, or even the flu.

There was medicine for leukemia to make Aimi get better, but the medicine took a long time to work. Aimi was going to be sick all year, at least. And the medicine Aimi needed to make her get better also made her feel worse. Sometimes she could be at home, but a lot of the time, she needed to be in the hospital, the way she was now.

And everything was different now. Mom and Dad were always tired and worried. The house was messy, and no one cooked anymore, the family just ate take-out fast food. They never did anything fun together, the way they used to. And now, Keiko couldn't even have a birthday party. All because of Aimi.

"It's just not fair!" Keiko shouted.

Suddenly, the black cloud of ugly feeling was growing inside her again, pushing its way out through her mouth, filling up her arms and legs, hands and feet, as though she had a tornado inside her.

Keiko picked up her pillow and threw it on the floor. Then she kicked the chair beside her desk. It fell to the floor with a BANG! She shoved the books on the desk onto the floor beside the chair. "I don't NEED you!" she screamed at them. "Mom and Dad don't care if I get bad grades now!"

Next, she grabbed her stuffed animals—Hoshi, the wise brown bear who had been her friend since she was little; Lady, the long yellow snake; and Jake, the soft, furry moose—and threw them against the wall. "I don't need you either!"

They dropped to the floor, looking sad and confused, but Keiko didn't care. The tornado in her arms and legs was still whirling around. She could hear it coming out of her mouth in one long, angry shout she didn't think would ever end.

And then she felt her mother's arms come around her. "Shh, Keiko, shh," Mom said.

Her mother held her tight, and the tornado spun more slowly. Then it stopped. When it had disappeared, Keiko suddenly felt scared and sad. She started to cry.

"I'm sorry, Mom," she whispered.

"It's okay, Keiko," her mother said. "I don't blame you for being upset."

Keiko sniffed back her tears and looked up at her mom. "You're not mad at me?"

Her mom shook her head. Keiko could see she was crying too, though. Keiko remembered what her grandma was always saying: "You have to be a big girl and help your mother now, Keiko. Don't give her any more worry than what she has already."

"I'm sorry," Keiko said again, feeling guilty. "I don't want to make you worry."

Her mom gave a shaky little laugh. "Keiko, you didn't do anything to make me worry. In fact, I'd be worried about you if you weren't upset. What you're feeling is perfectly normal. I feel the same way. So does Dad. It's NOT fair that Aimi's sick. It makes us mad and scared and frustrated, all at the same time. We miss the way things used to be. We're tired of being tired and sad. We're sick of never having any fun. We just want to go back to being a family again."

Keiko stared at her mother for a moment. Then she pulled away and picked up Hoshi from the floor. She had a question she wanted to ask her mom, a question she'd been thinking about for a long time but that she'd been scared to ask. She didn't know if she was brave enough to ask it even now.

"Mom?" Hoshi's wise furry face looked up at her, giving her courage. But Keiko didn't know if she wanted to know the answer to her question, even if she could bring herself to ask it.

Her mother knelt beside her. "What, Keiko?"

Keiko made herself say the words in a rush. "Is Aimi going to die?"

"Oh, Keiko. No. She's not going to die."

Keiko searched her mom's face. "You promise?"

Her mother looked sad. "I can't promise that, Keiko. But I don't think she will die. The doctors think they can make her better. It will just take a while."

Keiko thought about her mother's words. They weren't as good as what she'd hoped to hear, but they weren't as bad either. "Will Aimi always be sick?" Keiko asked. "Will she ever be back to normal?"

Her mom smiled. "Yes, she will. The treatment for leukemia takes a long time. But one day this will be over. One day, Aimi will be better."

Keiko woke up early on her birthday. She lay in bed, looking at the dress that hung from her closet door. It was long and purple and covered with lace, and she was going to wear it to the hospital for her birthday party. She had a big velvet hat to wear with it and long strings of pearls and an enormous ring that looked like Grandma's diamond. And there was a red silk dress covered with shiny stuff for Aimi to wear, with a matching floppy hat. Mom had bought the clothes at the secondhand store, and today, they were going to celebrate Keiko's birthday at the hospital, with Aimi.

A sound at her door, made Keiko turn her head. "Surprise!"

At first Keiko didn't recognize the round bald head that appeared in her doorway. Somehow, she always forgot that the medicine Aimi had to take for the leukemia had made her hair fall out. Then Keiko shouted, "Aimi! What are you doing here?"

Aimi came and sat on her bed. "Dad got permission for me to come home just for today, just for your birthday. You can't have a party in a hospital room, not a good party. And the doctor said I was doing okay. That if I didn't get too tired, it wouldn't hurt me."

Keiko stared at her big sister. She didn't look like herself, and Keiko could see that just walking across the floor to her bed had tired Aimi out. But she still sounded the same. She sounded just like Aimi.

"Mom's making tea and muffins," Aimi said. "Come on. Let's get dressed up." She picked up the floppy red hat and giggled. "At least this will cover up my silly bald head. How do I look?"

Keiko scrambled out of bed and reached for the purple dress. "You're beautiful, Aimi."

Aimi sank back on the bed while Keiko got dressed. "You're beautiful too, Keiko," she said. "Happy birthday!"

Keiko smiled at her sister. Life felt better already, just having Aimi here. Even if she was bald and tired and pale.

Later, when Mom and Dad, Grandma, and Aimi had sung happy birthday, and Mom had cut the cake, Keiko looked around the table at her family. "This," she said, "is the best birthday I ever had."

## It's Not Fair

By now, you've realized that not everything in life is fair. Your friends have better toys, you didn't get to go on that awesome vacation to California, and your bedtime is still way earlier than you'd like. But having a sick sibling is the ultimate unfair!

If you have a brother or a sister who is seriously sick, it changes your entire world. Suddenly, your parents aren't always around, you're getting less attention, and you have to spend half your time in the hospital visiting your sibling. Not to mention the fact that you're really scared for your sibling, and are unsure what's going to happen in the future. How is a kid supposed to deal with all this? It's not easy.

## Why Is My Sibling Sick?

In the story, Keiko's sister had leukemia, a type of blood disease. Leukemia is a form of cancer, which is the leading cause of death (behind accidents) of children under the age of fourteen. Out of all the types of cancer that children suffer from, leukemia is the most common. Fortunately, in the past few decades, there have been so many medical advances that the

Scientists are working hard to find cures for cancer and other diseases that affect children.

survival rate for childhood cancer is getting better and better. Today, about 16 out of every 100,000 kids are diagnosed with cancer, but only 3 out of every 100,000 die.

## Where You Fit In

### Understand the Word

Often, when a person has cancer, she undergoes a treatment called **chemotherapy**. It involves using chemicals to kill cancer cells, and it can leave the patient weak and bald.

Of those 16 out of 100,000 children who have cancer, many have brothers and sisters who are not sick. While they are getting **chemotherapy**, living in the hospital, and growing weaker, their siblings are also going through a rough time. They aren't sick with a serious disease like cancer, but it's definitely tough living with a sibling who does.

If you have a sibling with a serious illness, then you might feel pushed to the side. Your brother or sister is getting all the attention now, and your parents are too worried and distracted to spend much time with you when they aren't with your sibling. Your life isn't at all like what it used to be. Maybe like Keiko you can't have a birthday party, or you have to stop going to soccer practice, or your dad forgets to pick you up from school. It seems like you've had to make so many sacrifices, and no one has even noticed.

## What You're Feeling

Like Keiko's mom said, it's perfectly normal to be upset when your sibling is sick. First, you have to worry about your sick brother or sister, and you might be really scared that he or she is going to die. You're also probably worried about your mom and dad, who haven't been themselves lately. They seem tired all the time, and you might have seen them crying sometimes. Finally, you might be angry or upset that your life is so upside down right now. These are just a few of the emotions you could experience when a sibling gets sick. Here are some more:

- Fear. You might be afraid that someone else in your family will get sick too, whether or not your sibling's illness is **contagious**.
- Guilt. Some kids feel guilty because they're healthy and their siblings are not. You can still go to school, run around, and play with friends, even while your brother or sister is in

### Understand the Word

A disease that is **contagious** can be spread from one person to another.

the hospital. Other kids feel guilty because they think they somehow caused their siblings' illness by not getting along with them before they got sick.

• Sad. Lots of times, you could feel unhappy because your parents are paying so much attention to your sibling and not to you. You just want things back the way they were.

It's OK to feel sad if your sibling is sick. Spend some time alone, or talk to someone about what you're feeling.

- Resentment. You could just wish that everything was back the way it was before all this happened—and that resentment might come out at your parents, at your sibling who is sick, at God, or at life in general.
- Lonely. Not having your sibling around all the time can make you lonely, especially if you were close and you were used to playing together all the time. Your parents will be around less, too, so that makes you feel lonely also. You may feel as though having a serious illness in the family makes you different from the rest of your friends now, and you may think no one understands what you're going through.

## What Your Parents Are Feeling

You're feeling all sorts of emotions, and so are your parents. They're undoubtedly very upset and sad that one of their children is seriously ill and in the hospital. It's hard for them to deal with this too, so you should give them a little slack.

Sometimes your parents might yell at you more than they used to. They might be tired all the time and not up for playing with you or cooking you dinner, or they might frequently cry or worry out loud. None of this has to do with you. It's just as hard for grownups to deal with sickness as it is for children. Your parents are doing the best they can, but they can't always be perfect. Let them know that you're there for them, but that you want them to be there for you, too. You're in this as a family, and you should be helping each other through your sibling's illness.

## Changes at Home

In the story, Keiko's home life changed a lot. Her father wasn't home when she returned from school, she couldn't invite friends over for her birthday, and she had to eat fast food all the time. Having a sick sibling means your parents don't have as much time to run a normal household. Cooking and cleaning suddenly seem less important than making sure your brother or sister gets better as soon as possible.

As hard as it sounds, you just have to get used to living differently at home, at least for a little while. You unfortunately can't change the fact that your sibling is sick, so you have to learn to live with the changes that brings to your life at home.

Things change around the house once a member of the family gets sick. Dishes are left unwashed, dirty laundry piles up, and the lawn doesn't get mowed.

However, you should still expect to feel like a family. If your parents aren't paying any attention to you, or they forget to give you meals or take care of you, that's not okay. You're their child, too, and you have the right to live as normal a life as they can provide for you under these conditions. Let your parents know how you feel if you think something is wrong, or let another adult know who can talk to your parents for you.

## Understand the Word

To **disrupt** something is to throw it into disorder, to cause confusion, and to interrupt.

# Changes in Your Behavior

Having a sick sibling can affect you more than you think. Besides all those emotions it stirs up, it can also change your behavior. Some kids feel the need to act out on their anger over their siblings' illness. They get into fights at school, or attack the furniture in their room, like Keiko did. Sometimes this can be healthy, if it's directed in a positive way. Beating up a pillow is a good way to let out your anger—but beating up another kid is definitely not!

All that worry and stress can also **disrupt** your sleep. It's hard to fall asleep when you're so upset all the time, so you may find it hard to go to sleep at night, and you might always wake up tired. Other times, you have to visit the hospital at odd hours to visit your sick sibling, so you get less sleep during the night, and you may have to take more naps during the day.

You could notice that your grades at school change, too. Sometimes having to deal with a sick sibling causes kids to do worse at school. They don't have time to do homework, they miss school days so that they can take their sibling to the hospital or doctor's appointments, and they aren't motivated enough anymore to study and get good grades. On the other hand, other kids end up doing better at school, because they use schoolwork to take their minds off their situation at home. Everyone is different.

## Make It Better: Talk About It

Having a sick sibling is awful, but there are things that you and your family can do to make things a little better.

Most important is to keep talking to your parents. Once Keiko talked to her mom about her feelings, she felt a little better. Her mom probably felt better too. If your parents don't know you're upset, worried, or lonely, then they can't help you until they do know. It's

Talk to your parents, or someone else you trust. You'll make each other feel better.

also important that your parents tell you what's going on with your sick sibling. They shouldn't keep you in the dark if you want to know what disease your brother or sister has, whether he or she will live, and how he or she is doing in the hospital. If you know as much as you need to about the situation, you might not be so **anxious** about it. No matter how bad things are, the more you understand, the better you can cope with it.

Just having normal conversations with your parents is important too. Your sibling is sick, but you're still living your life. Tell your parents about what you're doing at school, something funny your friends told you, or about a new movie you want to see. Not everything has to change when your sibling is sick.

If you have other siblings who aren't sick, you should also talk to them about what they're going through. It helps to talk about what's going on with someone close to your own age. Your parents want to help you, but sometimes they just don't understand what you're feeling, no matter how hard you try to tell them. Talk to your sick sibling, too. He's still the same person he

### Understand the Word

If you are anxious, you are very worried about something and are uneasy and apprehensive.

was before he got sick, and he would probably appreciate knowing that you're there for him and that you still love him. If you're feeling scared, angry, lonely, and confused, image what he's feeling!

You might be scared of your brother or sister now that he or she is bald, weak, and in a hospital gown—but underneath it all, that's still your brother or sister.

## Make It Better: Have Fun

You don't have to be stressed out and worried all the time. Take some time to have fun, and you'll feel much better about the world. It's not good to be upset constantly, and no one will think badly of you if you laugh and have some fun once in a while, even if your sibling is sick.

Your parents should let you hang out with friends still, even if they can't come over to your house. Make time to see people you care about so that you don't get too overwhelmed with what's happening in your family.

Getting some exercise will also help you deal with your sibling's illness. Exercise makes people feel better because it releases good chemicals in our brains. Take time to run around with friends, play a game outside, or go sledding (whatever activity you think is fun). The activity will take your mind off your problems, and make you feel better.

## Make It Better: Help Your Sibling

If your sibling is ill, you might feel pretty helpless. Your sister is lying in a hospital bed, with tubes attached to her arms, and a sad look on her face. You feel out of control of the situation, and maybe you feel pretty hopeless. You can get rid of some of that feeling by getting your parents to include you in the care and treatment of your sibling. You can't be a doctor or a nurse, but you can help out in small ways. Go to the hospital to cheer up your sibling by reading to her or watching her favorite movie. Make him something special so he knows you care. Get her friends to write cards and send flowers. Small gestures that make your sibling smile will make you feel better—and you'll be doing something to help him feel better too.

## Outside Help

Sometimes you just need some extra help to get through such a tough experience. That's entirely okay. It doesn't mean you're weak, just that you're understandably having a hard time dealing with your sibling's illness, and all the changes that come along with it.

Ask your parents to search around for a sibling counseling group, a workshop for siblings or families of sick kids, or other people you could talk to. Hospitals often have programs already set up for kids like you. People there will know what you're going through, and they can help you work through it.

## Understand the Word

A **psychiatrist** is a doctor who is trained to diagnose, treat, and prevent mental illness. Psychiatrists have to go through many years of training before they can help people.

You could also go see a **psychiatrist**, who specializes in talking to children. Psychiatrists are trained to help kids like you, and they will take the time to listen to what you have to say. They'll even give you suggestions on how to deal with everything you're feeling and all the changes you've had to go through.

At school, you could talk to a counselor, whose job it is to talk to students like you. Ask a teacher how you can make an appointment with your counselor if you don't already know how to find him or her.

# After Sickness

Sooner or later, your sibling won't be sick anymore. Hopefully, they will get better and can come home before too long. Don't expect that everything will go right back to normal, because it will take some time before things settle down. You'll probably slowly go back to your old routines, once your sibling is truly better, but it will take a while. You've spent so long worrying about your life and about your family, so just focus on being happy that everyone is back together.

You also have to be prepared for a worse outcome. If your sibling has cancer, then there is a possibility that he or she could die. Your parents should let you know how your sibling is doing, and whether or not they expect him to get better or worse. If you face whatever happens as a family, you'll all get through it eventually.

No matter what happens, life isn't great right now. But it will be. You can't be sad forever, and you'll slowly get back to normal. Remember that you have to keep living your own life, and that there are lots of people who want to help you through your sibling's illness. Don't be afraid to take their help. You deserve all the help you can get!

# Questions to Think About

1. Keiko feels as though she has a "tornado" inside her. Have you ever felt like that? What other words could you use to describe feelings like that?

2. Why do you think Keiko felt as though this was her best birthday ever?

3. What things in your life don't seem fair? Do you think everyone has certain things they have to face that aren't fair?

4. What do you think will happen next in this story? What will be hard for Keiko to handle? What will make her happy?

## Further Reading

Duncan, Debbie. *When Molly Was in the Hospital.* New York: Raeve, 2000.

McVicker, Ellen. *Butterfly Kisses and Wishes on Wings: When Someone You Love Has Cancer.* Self, 2007.

Middendorf, Frances. *What About Me? When Brothers and Sisters Get Sick.* New York: Magination, 2004.

## *Find Out More on the Internet*

National Cancer Institute: When Someone in Your Family Has Cancer
www.cancer.gov/Templates/doc.aspx?viewid = 96338d5d-d432-41e3-a1ff-7d0adb4ae8bd

Sibling Support Project
www.siblingsupport.org

Super Sib
www.supersibs.org

The websites listed on this page were active at the time of publication. The publisher is not responsible for websites that have changed their address or discontinued operation since the date of publication. The publisher will review and update the websites upon each reprint.

# Index

# Picture Credits

## About the Authors

Sheila Stewart has written several dozen books for young people, both fiction and nonfiction, although she especially enjoys writing fiction. She has a master's degree in English and now works as a writer and editor. She lives with her two children in a house overflowing with books, in the Southern Tier of New York State.

Rae Simons is a freelance author who has written numerous educational books for children and young adults. She also has degrees in psychology and special education, and she has worked with children encountering a range of troubles in their lives.

## About the Consultant

Cindy Croft, M.A. Ed., is Director of the Center for Inclusive Child Care, a state-funded program with support from the McKnight Foundation, that creates, promotes, and supports pathways to successful inclusive care for all children. Its goal is inclusion and retention of children with disabilities and behavioral challenges in community child care settings. Cindy Croft is also on the faculty at Concordia University, where she teaches courses on young children with special needs and the emotional growth of young children. She is the author of several books, including *The Six Keys: Strategies for Promoting Children's Mental Health*.